The Love Test

Where Do You Stand?

We talk a lot above loving people but do
we really display love? Is your love genuine?
Want to find out? Take the love test.

William E. Bacote

ISBN 978-1-0980-7899-7 (paperback)
ISBN 978-1-0980-7900-0 (digital)

Christian Faith Publishing, Inc.
832 Park Avenue
Meadville, PA 16335
www.christianfaithpublishing.com

Printed in the United States of America

CONTENTS

CHAPTER 1

Can You Pass the Love Test?

(Ephesians 3:14–19; Revelation 2:1–5;
Romans 13:8–9, 12:9–10; Proverbs 4:23)

For this cause I bow my knees unto the
Father of our Lord Jesus Christ,
Of whom the whole family in heaven and earth is named,
That he would grant you, according to the riches of his glory,
to be strengthened with might by his Spirit in the inner man;
That Christ may dwell in your hearts by faith; that
ye, being rooted and grounded in love,
May be able to comprehend with all saints what is
the breadth, and length, and depth, and height;
And to know the love of Christ, which passeth knowledge,
that ye might be filled with all the fullness of God
—Ephesians 3:14–19 (KJV)

How much does God love us? Ponder that question for a moment. Does God love us like our neighbor, friends, siblings, parents? Less than they do or more? No matter your answer, God loves us more than we can understand. In Ephesians 3:14–19, Paul prays that the church in Ephesus would know how much Christ loved them. Paul prayed that the church might know how wide, long, deep, and high is the love of Christ. Signifying that the love of Christ reaches to no end in all directions, that his love surrounds us and is unending.

Love is the foundation of everything that God does. God loves mankind so much that

- he made us just a little lower than the angels;
- he gave us dominion over his creation;
- while we were yet sinners, he sent his son into the world to die for us.

Those who have received Christ

- are seated in heavenly places;
- have eternal life;
- are more than conquers through him who has loved us.

Notice that Paul prayed that the Ephesians would be strong in their inner man. The inner man is the real you. Only by strengthening the inner man will we be able to pass the love test. The type of love Christ displayed cannot be achieved through human ability. In order to display that type of love, Christ must dwell in our hearts and his love must be rooted in us. Only then can we love the unloving, those that hate us, use, and despise us. The type of love God wants us to display is not to just love those that love us but to also love those who from the human perspective might not deserve it.

Paul's focus is on the inner man. We spend a lot of time and money on the outer man. We buy grooming products, clothes, and gym memberships. We go to the gym and work out faithfully—all to make the outer man appear better. But what about the inner man, the real you? How much of our time, effort, and money is spent on building him up? How faithful are we in prayer and Bible study? Do we take the time to memorize and meditate on Scripture? Without taking these steps, the Word of God will not become engrafted in our hearts and we will not be able to love others the way that God desires.

How important is it for us to love? Paul says in Romans 13:8–9 that we are not to owe anyone anything but to love one another and that by loving one another, we fulfill the law. In these verses Paul says that commandments six through ten, which deal with man's relationship to man, are met when we love our neighbor as we love ourselves. Instead of trying to keep a list of commands, if we just practice true love, the commandments will be taken care of. Well then, love is pretty important, isn't it?

Paul defines attributes of love in Romans 12:9–10 that should be on our test. These are:

- Love should be without dissimulation. Dissimulation means concealment. Love should not be hidden. It is to be displayed, not for your sake or to call attention to you, but for the sake of others.
- Love hates evil. It dislikes that which is wicked.
- Love holds onto that which is good. It likes things that are decent and respectable.
- Love makes one kindly affectioned one to another. That is to have warm friendship with one another.
- Love makes one honor another rather than self. That is to put the welfare of others above your own.

God wants us to love others, but he also wants us to love him. Do you know anyone that when they were first saved, they were on fire for God? But as time passed, their fire seemed to die out. They stopped spending quality time with God. Stopped coming to Bible study and church on a regular basis. We may wonder what happened to them. But be careful. What about us? We may be busy doing church work but not growing in love and the things of God. Just because we are in church doesn't mean the church is in us.

John, in Revelation 2:1–5, speaks on this situation. While addressing the church at Ephesus, God says although they are doing good works, he has something against them. What is it? That they have left their first love. That is, their love for God had waned. As a result, God calls them to remember, consider, how far they had fallen from their first place and to repent, to turn around and rekindle the love they first had for him. Passing the love test requires that we do not let our love for God diminish. It must remain strong.

Proverbs 4:3 says to keep our heart with all diligence for out of it are the issues of life. What does that have to do with love? What did Paul pray for the Ephesians? First, that Christ would dwell in their hearts and then that they would be rooted and grounded in love. What or who is in your heart matters. For what is in the heart will come out. With Christ in our hearts, we can display love. So be careful to guard your heart. Don't let anything in that will diminish your love for Christ or your love for others.

Key Points

1. God loves us more than we can understand.
2. Love is the foundation of everything that God does.
3. The inner man is the real you.
4. We spend a lot of time and money on the outer man rather than the inner man.

The Love Test

1. Are you strong in your inner man?
2. Do you love your neighbor as you love yourself?
3. Is your love hidden or on display?
4. Do you hate that which is evil?
5. Do you hold to that which is good?
6. Are you truly friendly?
7. Do you put the welfare of others above your own?
8. Do you love God as much as when you first met him?

CHAPTER 2

Modeling Love

(1 Corinthians 13:1–3; John 4:1–5, 6–9, 28–42)

Though I speak with the tongues of men and of angels, and have
not charity, I am become as sounding brass, or a tinkling cymbal.
And though I have the gift of prophecy, and understand all
mysteries, and all knowledge; and though I have all faith, so that
I could remove mountains, and have not charity, I am nothing.
And though I bestow all my goods to feed the
poor, and though I give my body to be burned, and
have not charity, it profiteth me nothing.
—1 Corinthians 13:1–3 (KJV)

The thirteenth chapter of 1 Corinthians is sometimes referred to
as the love chapter. Here, Paul gives us a description of what love
is and is not. In the KJV, Paul uses the word *charity*. Charity is giving love. Love is an action word. It is to be demonstrated. However,
sometimes our deeds look like love but are not. In the first three
verses of chapter 13, Paul provides examples of doing good things
but those things amounting to nothing because there was no love in
them. Love is essential.

I remember reading a story where a scientist decided to make
a great Christian. As he worked, he provided all the elements he
thought would make his creation the best Christian ever. He included

the elements Paul spoke of. His creation was a great speaker, had a vast amount of knowledge and understanding, and had great faith. But in the end, the scientist realized that instead of creating this great Christian, he had created a monster. How could this have happened? Because he omitted the key element in his creation. He left out love.

Whatever we do in life should be motivated by love. God has given the church, the body of Christ, the ministry of reconciliation. We are to restore relationship between God and man. This is done by leading people to Christ. How can I lead someone to Christ? How can I help restore someone's relationship with God? You may think, "I am not a preacher or a deacon. What can I do or say?" All you need to lead people to Christ is love.

Jesus is to be our example. He said we are to do the things that he did. One of the things that Jesus did was love. Jesus modeled love in John chapter 4.

John 4:1–5 tells us that as Jesus left Judaea, he had a need to go through Samaria on his way to Galilee. During the time of Jesus, Palestine was divided into three regions. Judaea lie in the south and Galilee lie to the north. Samaria was between the two. When traveling between Judaea and Galilee, Jews normally took the long route around so as not to travel through Samaria. The Samaritans were looked down on by the Jews because they were descendants of Jews that had intermarried with the surrounding people. So the two groups had little to do with one another.

But Jesus had a need to go through Samaria. What was that need? A woman and a people that needed to know him and be saved.

Verses 5 through 9 of the chapter tell us that once Jesus got to Sychar, a city in Samaria, he sat by a well. A Samaritan woman came to the well at noon to get water. Jesus struck up a conversation with the woman by asking for a cup of water. This conversation concerning natural water turned into a conversation about spiritual water. The woman came to believe that Jesus was the Christ because of this conversation.

John 4:28–42 tell us that the woman was so moved that she left her water pot (remember, she had come to draw water) and went into the city and told the men to come see a man who had told her all that she had done. So the men decided to go see.

In between the time the woman left and the men got to Jesus, Jesus talked to his disciples about the fields being ripe for harvest. He was speaking of the world being ready to receive salvation. He explained to them that men were the reapers that were to gather the harvest. That message is for us today. Our mission is to spread the Word, letting people know who Jesus is. Jesus's command was to make disciples.

The men arrived and talked with Jesus. Because of his words, they asked him to stay two days. He did and many believed.

We are to make disciples—followers. The Word is for everybody. It is the responsibility of the church to get the Word out. Somebody's future is dependent on us.

Vine's *Expository Dictionary of Biblical Words* says the following: "Christian love, whether exercised toward the brethren, or towards men generally, is not an impulse from the feelings, it does not always run with the natural inclinations, nor does it spend itself only upon those for whom some affinity is discovered."[1]

Doesn't that describe what Jesus did? Jesus broke with custom, the normal routine, spoke to those who the Jews had no dealing with. Why? Out of love. He had need to go through Samaria, to those looked down on, to those on the fringes of society in order that they might be saved also.

The woman came to the well in the middle of the day, alone. In those days, drawing water from the town well was a social event for the women. Her coming alone suggests that she was rejected by the other women of the community.[2]

Does our love move us to reach out to the unlovable, those of a different culture, those that may not know Christ? Does our love

---

[1] W. E. Vine, *Vine's Expository Dictionary of Biblical Words* (Nashville. TN: Thomas Nelson Publishers, 1985).

[2] Lawrence O. Richards, *The Bible Reader's Companion* (Baltimore, MD: Halo Press, 1991).

move us to the point of having a need to reach those that others bypass? Jesus's love did and so should ours.

I heard the late Rick Majerus, a former college basketball coach, speak at a conference I attended. And one thing he said when talking about his relationship with his players has stuck with me: "Nobody cares how much you know, until they know how much you care."

It isn't about how much theological knowledge you have. It's about how much love you show people that makes the difference.

Key Points

1. Love is essential.
2. All you need to lead people to Christ is love.
3. Jesus modeled love.

The Love Test

1. Do you do good deeds out of love?
2. Does your love motivate you to reach out to all that do not know Jesus or only to those like you?

CHAPTER 3

Men and Women of Love
Make a Better Church

For God so loved the world that he gave his one
and only son, that whoever believes in him
shall not perish but have eternal life.

—John 3:16 (NIV)

What is the church? The church is not a building. It is a people called out by God. Men and women who are to be God's ambassadors or representatives in the earth. An ambassador speaks for the one that sent him. The church is not only to proclaim the goodness of God, but it is to model it also. The Bible is a story of God's love for his creation. If the church is to be what God intended, it needs to be composed of men and women of love.

Whatever you love, you will support. The first part of John 3:16 says God loved. The Greek word used here for loved is *agapao*. It means to love in a social or moral sense.[3] *Phileo*, another Greek word translated as love, means to love as a friend. That is to have affection for, a personal attachment as a matter of sentiment of feeling. Agapao

---

[3] James Strong, *The New Strong's Exhaustive Concordance of the Bible* (Nashville, TN: Thomas Nelson Publishers, 1995, 1996).

has a wider concept. It denotes the judgment and deliberate assent of the will as a matter of principle, duty, and decorum.[4] Simply put, it means a love that is by choice.

The verse says God loved the world. The world here in the Greek is *kosmos*, meaning, his creation including its inhabitants.[5] This love is not based on what the inhabitants did but from a choice God made. So the church, as God's representatives, should choose to love his creation. This includes the environment as well as including all of its inhabitants.

Remember that whatever we love, we will support. God loves us so much that he gave his only son to die for us. That was an awesome cost to God for making eternal life available to humankind. When we love, we don't mind giving to that which is loved. Jesus died for us, so the least we can do is to live for him.

Because God loves us and we have received his love, we are to share this message with the rest of the world. Why? So that they too might believe in Jesus.

The Greek word used here is *pisteuo*, which means to have faith in or with respect to a person or thing. Here it means to entrust one's spiritual well-being to Christ.[6] Since we have entrusted our future to Christ, we should want others to have what we have. What is it that we have? Assurance of eternal life.

The last portion of the verse says they that believe shall not perish but have eternal life. Perish means to destroy fully. We should have enough love that we do not want to see any die much less fully destroyed. What we should desire for all is everlasting life which comes through putting our trust in Christ. The world needs to know that escape from judgment and the possession of eternal life can be a present reality.

---

4   Ibid.
5   Ibid.
6   Ibid.

How has God shown his love for us?

- He sent his only son into the world to die for us.
- God chose to love sinners.
- God expressed his love through self-sacrifice.

Our churches will be better when the people in the church are directed by love. Then we will model the love of God by choosing to love others and carry the message that eternal life is in Christ Jesus to a lost world. The church is the body of Christ. If we love God, we will support the church and its directive from Christ, which is to seek the lost and make disciples. It is love that enables us to embark on this endeavor. Without it, the church will not be what God intended it to be. It needs men and women of love.

Key Points

1. Whatever you love, you will support.
2. Love is by choice.

The Love Test

1. Do you support your church? If so, how?
2. Do you choose to love when you feel others may not deserve your love?

CHAPTER 4

Stewardship: The Proof of Your Love

(Psalm 24:1; Genesis 1:1; Matthew 6:33)

The earth is the LORD's, and the fullness thereof;
the world, and they that dwell therein.

—Psalm 24:1 (KJV)

What is a steward? A steward is one who manages someone else's property for them. As stewards, we are to handle the owner's possessions in accordance to his desires, not ours.

Suppose I owned an apartment building. I bought the building to rent units to people as their place of habitation. But rather than me renting the units, I hired you to do that. I would expect you to find tenants, collect the rent, keep the property in a livable condition, etc. As a faithful steward, you would perform these duties. You would not leave the building vacant or put it in use for some other endeavor.

Dave Ramsey defines stewardship as managing God's blessings, God's ways, for God's glory. In our example, there would be something else I expected as owner. I would expect you, as a steward, to provide me with whatever portion of the income that I asked for when we agreed. As a steward, you cannot keep everything for yourself. Stewardship is manifested in giving. As my steward over the building, I would expect you to make sure the units were well maintained, basic needs were provided the tenants, and the building kept in a position where people would want to live there. Thus the stewards give or provide.

Let's briefly look at some principles for stewards of God's kingdom.

First, we must learn what God expects of us. Do you know what God expects of you? If not, how can you find out? By prayer, fasting, and submitting to the leadership of the pastor.

Prayer is communicating with God. We talk to him. Tell him about our problems and what we want. But how often do we ask him what does he want from us? What is it that he wants us to do? We sometimes ask God to bless our plans, but how often do we ask him what our plan should be? If we are truthful, our prayer life is often one-sided. We talk to God but don't wait to hear from him. Prayer should not be a monologue, when only one party speaks, but a dialogue where God speaks also. In prayer, ask God what he expects of you. Give him the opportunity to answer. He may speak to you directly, direct you to Scripture, and/or direct someone to you to provide confirmation.

Sometimes your praying may need to be accompanied with fasting. Fasting is a temporary denial of something that is in itself good, like food, in order to intensify our expression of need for something greater. That is, God and his work in our lives. Fasting helps us learn to control our physical bodies and minds. God speaks to us through our spirits and the Word, and fasting helps us break through those areas that might be hindering us from hearing from God. Fasting is sacrifice of our personal will unto God.

You can find out what God expects of you by sitting under and submitting to the leadership of your pastor. If you are not in a Bible-believing, Bible-teaching church, then get into one. The pastor is there to teach and guide you. He or she may recognize gifts in you and be able to help you develop those gifts so that you can function at the level that God wants you to. God has not gifted us just because. It is his investment in us, and he expects a return on his investment.

Secondly, we must develop compassion for the lost. The Bible is God's story of saving the lost after the fall of mankind. Remember Jesus seeing the multiples had compassion on them. If God is concerned about the lost, then we should be concerned about the lost. As stewards, our objective is to partner with the owner to meet his objective. So we are to show kindness to the lost and care for them as our capabilities allow. We should not be cold but loving so as to draw them to God.

Third, we must get our priorities in order. At the end of Matthew 6, Jesus talks about all the things that unbelievers seek after. And to be honest, they are things we seek after also. But in verse 33, he said to seek first the kingdom of God and all the other things we seek will be added. So our first priority is God.

After God comes our immediate family (spouse then children). The family was the first institution that God created. It is not to be neglected due to misplaced priorities. The Scripture says one that does not take care of his family is worse than an infidel. Your family does not have the proper priority if you don't take time to talk to them or you do not involve them in important decisions. You can show they are a priority by taking special occasions—anniversaries, birthdays, school events, etc.—seriously. Making time for family creates a sense of belonging and helps develop common values and beliefs.

Your profession or business priorities should come after these. Your business work is important but not as important as God and family. If you keep your priorities in the right order, the other things will come.

Next, recognize that God is the owner. Psalm 24:1 supports what we explored in chapter 3 (also Exodus 9:29 and Job 41:11). It tells us of God's lordship over the world. Genesis 1:1 tells us that God created the heaven and the earth. God owns everything, even us. As the owner, he has the right to do whatever he wishes with his possessions.

So it is with God and us. He is the owner of everything. We as stewards are to use his possessions and care for them as he desires. Which means we are to protect and expand the assets of God. God made man stewards in Genesis 1:26–28. We are not owners but stewards. As such, we must move from ownership thinking to thinking of ourselves as stewards. Otherwise, we will be in conflict with the true owner: God.

Be faithful over what you already have. If you are not faithful over a little, you will not be faithful with a lot. Recall the parable of the talents. To the two that used what they already had, more was given. The one that did nothing with the little, lost that. God is looking for a return on his investment. You will receive more when you show you can handle what has already been given you. Don't despise small beginnings. They can lead to a bigger future.

Develop the right attitude about money and possessions. God doesn't mind you having things. He just doesn't want the things to have you. The Bible doesn't say money is the root of all evil. But it does say that the *love* of money is the root of all evil. Don't concentrate on storing up earthly treasure. Instead, focus on heavenly treasure.

But don't fall for Satan's trap in thinking that it is spiritual to be poor. We need resources in order to help others. If you don't have enough, how can you help someone else? Money is neither good nor evil. It is just a tool. It is your perspective and how you use it that makes the difference.

Lastly, learn to make your money grow. You can do that through offerings and investments. The Bible is full of good financial advice. It tells us to give God, the owner, his share first. God promises to provide for us and not holding back on giving to him, displays our trust in him. The Bible also tells us that we can give and receive more, but those that are stingy and try to hold on to what they have will lose it.

The Bible also tells us to be wise and work while we can and to store something up for when we can't. It implores us to look at the animal world, be like the ant for example. Give God first. Pay yourself (invest) next. Investing is a way to multiply the resources God has given us to provide for our current and future needs. It is also a means to increase what we have available to impact God's kingdom.

Key Points

1. A steward is one who manages someone else's property.
2. Stewardship is manifested in giving.

3. Stewardship principles.
   a) Learn what God expects of us.
   b) Develop compassion for the lost.
   c) Get your priorities in order.
   d) Recognize that God is the owner.
   e) Be faithful over what you already have.
   f) Develop the right attitude about money and possessions.
   g) Learn to make your money grow.

The Love Test

1. Are you a good steward?
2. Do you give to God and others?
3. What do you do for the lost?
4. What are your priorities?

CHAPTER 5

Love Has a Price Tag?

(Genesis 29:13–20; 1 John 4:7–8, 18; 1 Corinthians 13:13)

And it came to pass, when Laban heard the tidings
of Jacob his sister's son, that he ran to meet him, and
embraced him, and kissed him, and brought him to
his house. And he told Laban all these things.
And Laban said to him, Surely thou art my bone and my
flesh. And he abode with him the space of a month.
And Laban said unto Jacob, Because thou art my
brother, shouldest thou therefore serve me for
nought? tell me; what shall thy wages be?
And Laban had two daughters: the name of the elder
was Leah, and the name of the younger was Rachel.
Leah was tender eyed; but Rachel was beautiful and well-favoured.
And Jacob loved Rachel; and said, I will serve thee
seven years for Rachel thy younger daughter.
And Laban said, It is better that I give her to thee, than
that I should give her to another man: abide with me.
And Jacob served seven years for Rachel; and they seemed
unto him but a few days, for the love he had for her.
—Genesis 29:13–20 (KJV)

Who likes to get something for free? We all do. But I remember my father saying, things that come easy aren't worth much. The important things, you have to work for. The same applies to love. True love has a price tag. It will cost you something.

In the above verses from Genesis 29, we see Jacob. The scripture tells us that he loved Rachel. As a result, he was willing to work for Laban for seven years in order to have her. Notice that it was Jacob that set the time period, not Laban. Jacob didn't say one week, one month, or even one year—but seven years. And verse 20 said although it was seven years, it seemed like days. Why? Because he loved her.

I remember when my brother got married, I was in junior high school. He and his wife stayed with my parents and me at first. My sister-in-law decided she was going to cook dinner for everyone. When I got home from school, my mother met me at the door. She said, "Eat it and you better not say a word."

The meal was horrible. I don't think anything was good. I ate it without saying a word because my mother commanded me to. Now my sister-in-law knew how to cook. It was just a case of nerves and nothing came out right.

Some years later, when I was dating Debra, now my wife, she decided to cook a meal for me. She was living with her parents and when I got there, she set the table and fixed my plate. Another meal gone bad. The food was burnt. Again, it was a case of nerves as she was a good cook.

Like in the case with my sister-in-law's first meal, I sat there and ate it. But something was different this time. I didn't eat the food because someone made me do it. I didn't withhold my complaints because someone told me not to say anything. I did it out of love. I didn't want her to feel bad. And to me, although it was burnt, it wasn't too bad.

Debra later told me that after I left, her mother said, "That boy must really love you to eat that." And that her mother had thrown out the food that remained. They wouldn't eat it! What made the difference in my attitude and perspective in the two situations? In the latter, it was all about love.

One of my former pastors told the story of meeting his wife while they were in college. He didn't have much money and wanted to take her out. He sold blood in order to get enough money to take her out to eat.

Each of the cases above, Jacob's, mine, my former pastor's, share some things in common. Each case cost us something. Jacob had worked seven years. I ate a bad meal and did not complain. My pastor sold his blood. But in each case, the cost was gladly paid out of love.

Love is about relationship. First John 4:7 tells us that love is of God. In order to be able to truly love others, we need to have a relationship with God. That same verse tells us to love one another. You see, the love of God is to be shown through love of one another. And when we have a relationship with someone, when we make a connection, it becomes easier for us to love them. In the cases of the two meals, I knew my sister-in-law but not like I knew Debra. I had not spent as much time with her, getting to know her, as I had with Debra. Therefore, it was easier for me to overlook what may have been a fault and display love. There was more of a relationship.

The key to displaying love is knowing God. According to 1 John 4:8, you can't know God if you don't love. The Amplified Bible puts it this way, "He who does not love has not become acquainted with God." To be acquainted means to have a personal knowledge of a thing or person. Some of us know about God but don't have a personal knowledge of him. That is why we find it difficult to love. We have yet to develop a personal relationship with God.

If we are honest, sometimes we find it difficult to love because of our experiences. We showed love to someone and maybe they hurt us in return. So we are afraid to show love again. But 1 John 4:18 says that "perfect love casteth out fear." Perfect here does not mean without mistake but complete. The Amplified says full-grown. It also says that when we fear, we have not reached the full maturity of love. So love is a process that we grow into. When fear causes us not to love, recognize and acknowledge it. Then decide to overcome it and love anyway. Remember, we were not saved until we acknowledged we needed a savior.

What moves us to display love? Below are four reasons or motivations for us to love:

1. God first loved us.
2. We owed a debt that we couldn't pay.
3. God gets the glory when the saints love one another.
4. The Bible commands us to love.

God first loved us. God loved us when we didn't love him (Romans 5:8). It is not unreasonable for us to love God. Look at all that he has done for us. He provides, protects, and saves us. So we should love him. But the great thing is God loved us first. Even when we did not acknowledge him, while we were yet sinners, God loved us. That should motivate us to love others, whether we feel like they deserve our love or not. Mankind had committed high treason and God still loved us. So we should demonstrate that same kind of love.

We owed a debt that we couldn't pay. We had disobeyed God. The penalty was death. We were all dead men walking. But God loved us so much in that while we were still sinners, he sent his son, Jesus, to pay the penalty for our sins. Jesus paid the debt owed. God's love had a price tag: the blood of his son.

God gets the glory when the saints love one another. The world is watching us. They are looking to see how we handle ourselves when the pressure is on or when we think no one is looking. When we do things the way that God would want us to, the love which Jesus modeled, the world notices and God gets the glory. Just keep on loving no matter what and give the glory to God.

The Bible commands us to love. Love is not optional for the Christian. It is a mandate, an order, from God. Remember the case of my sister-in-law's first meal she prepared for her new family? I ate it and did not complain, not because I wanted to but because my mother, the one in authority, told me to. God is the highest authority. He has commanded us to love, so do it even if we don't want to. If we practice love, it will become a natural part of what we do.

Paul wrote in 1 Corinthians 13:13 concerning faith, hope, and love. The *Amplified* defines each one.

Faith is the conviction and belief respecting man's relation to God and divine things. Hope is the joyful and confident expectation of eternal salvation while love is true affection for God and man, growing out of God's love for us and in us.

Paul says that love is greater than faith. Isn't that amazing? Faith can move mountains. Faith makes the impossible possible. Galatians 5:6 says that faith worketh by love. We seek to have more faith or stronger faith, but do we seek to have more love? Love needs to be the one thing in life we seek more than anything else.[7] Why is love so important? Without it, whatever we do or say has no lasting value.[8] Real love has life-changing power.

You see, the kind of love God wants us to give others is impossible to "manufacture" on our own. You might say that it is a "supernatural" love. It is a natural outflow of God's presence in our lives. According to Romans 5:5, the Holy Spirit fills our hearts with love. "If you feel your love for others is falling short of God's ideal, ask the Holy Spirit to strengthen you in this area. Your relationships with others will never be the same."[9]

Love Is/Does	Love Is Not/Does Not
patient	selfish
kind	hold grudges
quick to forgive	
looks for the best in others	

The God kind of love is patient. It will cause you to endure pain and trouble without complaining. You will not be easily provoked by others. You will be diligent and persevering in your love.

---

[7] Greg Laurie, *New Believer's Bible, New Testament, Wheaton* (IL: Tyndale House Publishers, Inc., 1996).

[8] Ibid.

[9] Ibid.

Love is kind. It shows itself through being sympathetic and friendly. It will cause you to be gentle and generous.

Love is quick to forgive. You will forgive before being asked for forgiveness.

Love looks for the best in others. It overlooks faults and sees the good.

Love is not selfish. *Webster's* defines selfish as "having such regard for one's own interests and advantage that the welfare of others becomes of less concern than is considered just."[10] In other words, love doesn't take advantage of others.

Love does not hold grudges. What is a grudge? It is a strong feeling of resentment or malice held against someone.[11]

Paul said that the greatest Christian virtue is love. But love has a price tag. How much are you willing to pay?

Key Points

1. Love is a relationship.
2. You can't know God if you don't love.
3. Perfect love casteth out fear.
4. Motivations to love.
   a) God first loved us.
   b) We owed a debt that we couldn't pay.
   c) God gets the glory when the saints love one another.
   d) The Bible commands us to love.
5. The greatest Christian virtue is love.

The Love Test

1. Do you know God?
2. Are you afraid to love others?

---

[10] David B. Guralnik, *Webster's New World Dictionary* (Nashville, TN: The World Publishing Company, 1973).
[11] Ibid.

CHAPTER 6

A Successful Marriage Relationship

(1 Corinthians 7:1–3; Exodus 22:16; Genesis
2:15–18; Ephesians 5:21–22)

Now concerning the things whereof ye wrote unto
me: It is good for a man not to touch a woman.
Nevertheless, to avoid fornication, let every man have his
own wife, and let every woman have her own husband.
Let the husband render unto the wife due benevolence:
and likewise also the wife unto the husband.
—1 Corinthians 7:1–3 (KJV)

We have talked about our love for God and how we are to love others. Now, let's focus on another area: marriage.

The church in Corinth had questions. Paul wrote 1 Corinthians as a response to their questions. One of the things they had questions about was marriage. In our focal verses above, Paul begins by saying, "It is good for a man not to touch a woman." But knowing the desires between the sexes, Paul says a man should have one wife and the woman one husband and neither should withhold themselves from the other. Keep these thoughts in mind as we discuss the idea of marriage.

It may seem that Paul begins by condemning marriage. But the thought behind his statement is that if you are unmarried, you can be more dedicated to God because you do not have to consider the needs of a spouse. But knowing that remaining single is not for all, he approves marriage between one man and one woman. But touching a woman can be looked at from another viewpoint also. There is an Old Testament principle of if you touch her, she is yours.

In Exodus 22:16, Moses wrote that if a man entices a woman and lies with her, then she is to be his wife. This was a principle that was practiced by our ancestors. Ever heard of shotgun weddings? That was when a female became pregnant out of wedlock and the male was forced to marry her, at gunpoint if necessary. I am not advocating shotgun weddings, but sex was designed to be between a husband and wife. So as Christians, we need to keep in our minds that if I touch her, she is mine.

This should not be a problem for Christians. Christians should live with a higher order. We are not to live as the world does. We should not do anything to bring disgrace to another person or to the body of Christ. As Christians we are to abstain from sex until we get married. That may be an old-fashioned idea, but all of God's rules are for our benefit. Your wedding night should be special. There should be anticipation. You ruin that when you don't wait.

Some say, "Oh, but I just fell head over heels in love for him or her." You don't fall in love; you grow in love. If you grow in love, you will grow in honor and respect for each other. You will hold one another in high regard and be considerate and want to maintain the good reputation of one another.

Your body is the temple of God. Sleeping around is not an option for Christians. When two people come together, the intent was for the two to become one. You become connected to the other person during sex. This connection follows you as it was intended for man and wife. Intention is the original plan or goal. In the book of Genesis, we see God's original plan. Let's look at intent in Genesis 2:15–18.

We see God placing Adam in the Garden of Eden. God gave him a job. He was to dress and keep the garden. In the Hebrew, according to Vine,[12] to dress means "to cover" and keep means "to

---

[12] W.E. Vine, *Vine's Expository Dictionary of Biblical Words.*

preserve." Then God gave him Eve as a helpmate because it was not good for him to be alone. From this we can see that the man is to dress, keep, cultivate, and guard the woman. Men, if you are not ready and willing to perform these duties, then you are not ready to marry her.

Although God said it was not good for the man to be alone, loneliness is the wrong reason to get married. Don't settle for less than God's best for you just because you are lonely. Don't forget to check for the worm before you bite the apple. What do I mean by that? Check for things that might be wrong. All that glitters is not gold.

Ladies, does he have a job? If the answer is no, that is a worm. Unless he lives in a major city, does he have a car? No, another worm. Watch how he treats his mother and sisters. Why? Because most likely, that is how he is going to treat you after you get married. Too many men get married thinking, "She is not going to change." Too many women get married thinking, "I can change him." Neither is realistic. We change as we grow, but no one can make anyone else change. If you fell in love or got married because you were lonely, change will be a problem, but if you continue to grow in love, you can handle change.

There are three kinds of marriage relationships: monogamous, polygamous, and common-law. Let's take a brief look at each.

Monogamous. One man to one woman. In a monogamous relationship, each partner is faithful to the other. A monogamous relationship is exclusive. Others are excluded. It is just for the two of you. Which means you are committed to one another. You may have heard both have to give 50 percent. But that is each giving half. To have a successful marriage, both have to give 100 percent, their all. This is the marriage for the Christian: husband and wife being fixed in the relationship, one-to-one, monogamy.

Polygamous. One man too many women. No, too is not misspelled. If you have more than one spouse, that is too many. Polygamy is the opposite of monogamy. In the Old Testament we see examples of polygamy. Abraham, David, and Solomon, all had more than one wife. But in the New Testament, we see one man and one wife.

Remember, Paul said, let every man have his own wife and every woman her own husband. In our society, polygamy is illegal. A bigamist (person with two wives) can go to jail.

But some have a polygamous relationship while having only one mate. They are two-timing their spouse. They are only married to one person but are having adulterous relationships. They may not go to jail for this, but this is criminal in the sight of God. Christians should not practice polygamy. Thy shall not commit adultery.

Common-law. Cohabitation without legal obligation, no guidelines. Commonly referred to as "shacking up." This is where couples want some of the benefits of marriage without the spiritual and legal obligations that come with marriage. There is no real commitment. I can leave whenever I choose. Some use the reasoning of "trying it out so I don't make a mistake in marriage." But statistics (*The Atlantic* March 20, 2014) say that couples that live together before marriage have a 33 percent higher rate of divorce than those who waited to live together until after they were married. I think the reason is that common-law does not have the emotional ties of real marriage. So common-law is not a real test of the marriage bond. It is kind of like playing a sport. Practice is different than playing in the game.

You see, marriage is the highest order of spiritual warfare. Marriage was ordained by God in the garden. Therefore, the devil hates it. The devil wants to come between you and your mate. Just like he came between Adam and Eve and caused the fall. Where there is no unity, there is no strength. That is why it is critical for spouses to be committed to each other. Playing house won't cut it. Ninety-nine and a half won't do.

There are three keys to a successful marriage relationship. They are submission, love, and sacrifice.

To submit is to fall under or obey. Ephesians 5:21–22 says that we are to submit to one another in reverence for God. It goes on to say that wives are to obey their husbands. God has placed the husband as the head of the home, but that does not make him the boss. He is to lead by example in love. Most women will not have a problem submitting to their husbands if he is following God. Recall Genesis 2. The man is to dress, keep, cultivate, and guard the woman.

She needs to feel secure and protected. She needs to know that her husband loves her and is committed to her. When the husband meets these needs, she has no problem in submitting to him as the head.

Another key is love. Both must love the other. In the prior chapter, we talked about what love is and isn't, what love does and does not do. Go and read the thirteenth chapter of 1 Corinthians in its entirety. Make note of what true love is and how it is displayed, such as love keeps no count of wrongs. Don't continuously bring up the negative things from the past. First Peter 4:8 says love covers a multitude of sins. Instead of focusing on the bad, focus on the good. Think on those things.

To sacrifice is to give up something important. It is to give of yourself for your spouse. Once you are married, it is no longer all about you. There is nothing wrong with expressing your desires and needs. We all have them. But do not neglect those of your spouse in order to get what you want. Both parties should be willing to make sacrifices for the other. I don't like baseball, but I will go to the game with him (at least occasionally) and go to a "chick" flick with her instead of going to the game.

The ability to sacrifice is what is missing in most marriages. "When you are not willing to make sacrifices, you send a message that you don't really love me. You may love what I do for you, but you really don't love me." Remember the sacrifice Jacob made for Rachel? How about the sacrifice Jesus made for us?

The marriage relationship mirrors that of Christ and the church. If we are to have successful marriages, we are going to have to submit to each other. We are going to have to display true love and be willing to make sacrifices for each other. Being fully committed to each other and in unity.

If you are not ready for all three, then you are not ready for marriage.

Key Points

1. You don't fall in love; you grow in love.
2. Your body is the temple of God.

3. There are three kinds of marriage relationships: monoga-mous, polygamous, common-law.
4. Where there is no unity, there is no strength.
5. Keys to a successful marriage relationship: submit, love, sacrifice.

The Love Test

1. Do you honor and respect your mate?
2. Are you in a monogamous relationship?
3. Do you submit to your mate?
4. Do you make sacrifices for your mate?

CHAPTER 7

God's Love Manifested

I am the true vine, and my Father is the gardener.
He cuts off every branch in me that bears no
fruit, while every branch that does bear fruit he
prunes so that it will be even more fruitful.
You are already clean because of the word I have spoken to you.
Remain in me, and I will remain in you. No branch can
bear fruit by itself; it must remain in the vine. Neither
can you bear fruit unless you remain in me.
I am the true vine; you are the branches. If a man
remains in me and I in him, he will bear much
fruit; apart from me you can do nothing.
If anyone does not remain in me, he is like a branch
that is thrown away and withers; such branches are
picked up, thrown into the fire and burned.
If you remain in me and my words remain in you,
ask whatever you wish, and it will be given you.
This is to my Father's glory, that you bear much
fruit, showing yourselves to be my disciples.
As the Father has loved me, so have I loved
you. Now remain in my love.
If you obey my commands, you will remain in my love, just as
I have obeyed my Father's commands and remain in his love.

I have told you this so that my joy may be in
you and that your joy may be complete.
My command is this: Love each other as I have loved you.
Greater love has no one than this, that he
lay down his life for his friends.
You are my friends if you do what I command.
I no longer call you servants, because a servant does not know his
master's business. Instead, I have called you friends, for everything
that I learned from my Father I have made known to you.
You did not choose me, but I chose you and appointed
you to go and bear fruit—fruit that will last. Then the
Father will give you whatever you ask in my name.
This is my command: Love each other.
—John 15:1–17 (NIV)

How are you doing on the love test? Do you think it is hard? Are you thinking, "How can I do all this?" It is impossible if we try to do it on our own, but our focal verses for this chapter provide the keys which will enable us to love.

Our text is in the middle of what is called the Farewell Discourse of Jesus. The content stretches from John 13–15. It was the night of his betrayal. In an upper room somewhere in Jerusalem, Jesus met with his disciples, washed their feet, instituted the Lord's Supper, predicted his betrayal and denial, and promised the Holy Spirit. The theme of the evening is love. In fact, love appears around forty-three times from John 13–21.

Go back and the read the verses again.

John 15:1–8

The relationship between Jesus and his followers is described as the relationship of the branches to a vine. The details of the imagery are easily discerned: God is the gardener and the one who does the pruning. Jesus is the true vine, and disciples are the branches. Vines produce fruit. The best fruit in the Christian experience is love. Jesus marked out two keys to the production of matchless love. The first is to abide (remain). The word *remain* appears eleven times in our text. The King James Version uses the word *abideth*, which means "to remain; to continue to be present." To love like Jesus, we must receive the love of Jesus. This is done best by constantly abiding in him. We must remain in the vine.

The second is to be pruned. The King James says *purgeth*. The Greek word for prunes also means cleans. The implication is to prune trees and vines from useless shoots to cleanse from impurity. In God's vineyard, it is not just the old, worn-out branches that get cut out. The healthy branches he also cuts back (literally lifts and separates). The goal in pruning is to make the branches even more productive.

Fruit refers to works. Our fruit is for others and the glory of God. The ultimate fruit is love.

John 15:9–17

The disciples proved their love by their obedience. We, in turn, prove our love for Christ by our obedience to him and receive his promise of abiding in him. Jesus got intimate in this section of our text. He spoke about the closeness he has with his Father, and he invites believers into that intimacy by being their friend. The Father loves the Son. The Son loves the disciples. The disciples love one another. This love involves sacrifice, but that thought is not oppressive. When love is in high gear, sacrifice is actually a joy. Is there a greater way to demonstrate love than through sacrifice?

We are surrounded with scriptures that encourage us to make love our highest priority. Matthew 22:37–38 tells us to love God with all we have, and that this is the first and great commandment. Jesus said if we love him, we will keep his commandments (John 14:15). Jesus says after loving God, the other great commandment is to love our neighbor as we love ourselves (Mark 12:28–31). Second Timothy 2:2 tells us to pursue love. Do I need to list more to show how important it is to love?

Jesus removed any awkward distance by calling those who love him and remain in him friends. There is a difference between a friend and a servant. Jesus said a servant doesn't know the master's business, but the disciples were friends because he told them everything he had learned from the Father. But there is another difference. Servants serve because they must. Friends serve because they want to serve.

Key Points

1. We prove ourselves to be disciples of Jesus when we love.
2. Disciples stay connected to the vine to bear fruit.
3. Jesus commanded us to love one another.
4. The keys to being able to love are:
   a) remain in Jesus, and
   b) allow Jesus to prune (cleanse) you.

The Love Test

1. Does your life display any evidence of love?
2. Is loving others a high priority for you?

CHAPTER 8

The Source of All Love

Beloved, let us love one another; for love [springs] from God, and
he who loves [his fellow men] is begotten (born) of God and is
coming (progressively) to know and understand God—to perceive
and recognize and get a better and clearer knowledge of Him.
He who does not love has not become acquainted with
God—does not and never did know Him; for God is love.
In this the love of God was made manifest (displayed), where we
are concerned, in that God sent His Son, the only begotten or
unique [Son], into the world so that we might live through Him.
In this is love, not that we loved God, but that He loved us and sent
His Son to be the propitiation (the atoning sacrifice) for our sins.
Beloved, if God loved us so [very much],
we also ought to love one another.
No man has at any time [yet] seen God. But if we love one
another, God abides (lives and remains) in us and His love
[that love which is essentially His] is brought to completion—
to its full maturity, runs its full course, is perfected—in us!
By this we come to know (perceive, recognize and understand)
that we abide (live and remain) in Him and He in us: because
He has given (imparted) to us of His (Holy) Spirit.
And [besides] we ourselves have seen [have deliberately
and steadfastly contemplated], bear witness that the
Father has sent the Son [as the] Savior of the world.

Any one who confesses (acknowledges, owns) that Jesus
is the Son of God, God abides (lives, makes His home) in
him, and he (abides, lives, makes his home) in God.
And we know (understand, recognize, are conscious of,
by observation and by experience), and believe (adhere
to and put faith in and rely on) the love God cherishes
for us. God is love, and he who dwells and continues
in God, and God dwells and continues in him.
In this [union and communion with Him] love is brought to
completion and attains perfection with us, that we may have
confidence for the day of judgment—with assurance and boldness
to face Him—because as He is, so are we in this world.
There is no fear in love—dread does not exist; but full-grown
(complete, perfect) love turns fear out of doors and expels every
trace of terror! For fear brings with it the thought of punishment,
and [so] he who is afraid has not reached the full maturity
of love—is not yet grown into love's complete perfection.
We love Him, because He first loved us.
—1 John 4:7–19 (AMP)

The scripture verses are a message concerning God's love and ours. In this chapter, we will consider differences and similarities between God's love and human love. Afterward, each of us should be motivated to demonstrate what it means to love others the way God loves us.

God is love and his love is very different than human love. How is God's love different? God loves unconditionally. The love of God is forgiving. God's love is sacrificial. God's love is also unselfish.

God loves unconditionally. God loves us no matter what. God's love is genuine. It is not based on feelings or emotions. He doesn't love us because we have fulfilled some requirement. God loves each of us, and we can see that in the Bible. First John 4:19 tells us that God loved us first. He loved us first and he will never stop.

The love of God is forgiving. Although we have been disobedient, God still loves. He not only gives us a second chance but a third, fourth, fifth… When we confess our sins, God forgives us and remembers our sin no more.

We, on the other hand, may not be so forgiving. We may be like Peter when he asked Jesus how many times we must forgive: seven times. Or is it "Fool me once shame on you, fool me twice, shame on me"? We like to keep count of others' wrongdoings as excuse not to love instead of being forgiving.

God's love is sacrificial. God loves us so much that he sent his son to die on our behalf. He made a way for a repayment of a debt that we could not pay. Yet many times we demand payment for a small debt and yet say we love.

God's love is unselfish. God's love thinks of others first. On the other hand, the flesh is selfish and self-centered. We love if it gets us something. We might ask, "What am I going to get out of it?

We humans tend to love the world and the things of the world instead of having the love of God within us (see 1 John 2:15). Not all human love is a reflection of God's love. That may make it difficult for some of us to comprehend how much God loves us and distorts our vision of true love. Are we able to love like God? No, not of ourselves, but we can once we die to self and allow God to live within us.

First John 4:11 is our key verse. If God loved us so much, then we ought to love one another. How much did God love? Verses 7–11 tell us, God so loved that he gave. God so loved that he sent. God so loved that he sacrificed. All of these mesh together to underline the gift of Christ on Calvary's cross.

What would be different about our community of faith if we truly showed love as the principal mark of true discipleship? Our churches would grow. People want to be a part of a community where people care about one another. We would have a greater impact on the community at large. We would put feet to our love by meeting the needs of the community instead of just talking about what needs to be done. When people know you care, they tend to be more willing to listen.

If God's love is supposed to compel us to love one another, what gets in the way? Are we too busy (selfish) with our own lives to take time to demonstrate love to others? Perhaps, we really don't care as long as our needs are met. Or is it that we really don't know how to love?

First John 4:12 says that no man has seen God. It is fundamentally true that no one has actually seen God with their natural eyes. Thus the question arises, "How does one truly see God?" We see God in his Son, but in reference to John's point, we see God in everyday life as we demonstrate true love toward one another.

Where does this love come from? God is the source of love. Without God in our hearts, we cannot love the way that God wants us to. Our love will be conditional, based on our emotions and feelings. We will put ourselves first when we have the ability to meet their needs even when we could easily meet them.

When we love others, we perfect or complete God's command to love as he, through Christ, has loved us. Remember this:

- God lives in his people through the Holy Spirit.
- Loving one another, the presence of the Spirit in us, and our confession of faith that Jesus is the Son of God are assurances that God abides in us and we in him.

In 1 John 4:16, John tells us that God is love. What does he mean? He means that love is an inseparable aspect of God's character, and God shows us what love is supposed to look like.

The reality of God's love among believers is a means of confidence on the Day of Judgment. Boldness means confidence among those of high rank. Are you confident that if you stood before God, he would say that you passed the love test?

In order to pass, our love has to be more like God's love than human love. Once we allow God's love to control our lives, it will grow and become complete. As a result, we will be able to come boldly before God's throne of judgment, confident that he will not cast us away.

In summary, what was John saying?

- Expressing love for one another is an outward sign of love for God.

- When we love or fail to love others, we demonstrate whether or not we truly love God.
- The more we understand God's great love for us, the more we are motivated to love him and that love will overflow in love for others.

In closing, see what Jesus said in John 13:34–35. Are you obeying his commandment? Do people know that you are a disciple without you telling them but by your actions? This is not a test that you cram for and then forget what you learned. Jesus said to keep on doing it. Can you pass the love test?

Key Points

1. If God loves us so much, then we ought to love one another.
2. God is the source of love.
3. Once we allow God's love to control our lives, it will grow and become complete.

The Love Test

1. Do you express love for others?
2. Do you keep an account of others' wrongdoings?
3. Can others see the love of God in you?
4. Do you fear the Day of Judgment?

BIBLIOGRAPHY

Guralnik, David B. *Webster's New World Dictionary.* Nashville, TN: The World Publishing Company, 1973.

Laurie, Greg. *New Believer's Bible, New Testament.* Wheaton, IL: Tyndale House Publishers, Inc., 1996.

Richards, Lawrence O. *The Bible Reader's Companion.* Baltimore, MD: Halo Press, 1991.

Strong, James. *The New Strong's Exhaustive Concordance of the Bible.* Nashville, TN: Thomas Nelson Publishers, 1995, 1996.

Vine, W. E. *Vine's Expository Dictionary of Biblical Words.* Nashville, TN: Thomas Nelson Publishers, 1985.

About the Author

William E. Bacote teaches in a manner that makes him easy to understand. He uses his gift of teaching to equip the saints for the work of the ministry. He has spoken at seminars, luncheons, Bible studies, and church services. He recognizes the voice of God and is an excellent teacher of the Word.

He has served his church as a Sunday school and Bible study teacher, Sunday school superintendent, Director of Christian Education, a deacon, and done prison ministry.

William is married to the former Debra Jeffery and is the father of three children: two daughters and a son. He is also a grandfather of three and has one great-granddaughter.

CPSIA information can be obtained
at www.ICGtesting.com
Printed in the USA
BVHW071333160621
609638BV00005B/410